Spiritual
Authority

Other books by David M. Adams.

The Bare Necessities of Faith.

Seek My Face - the biblical basis of seeking the Lord

Spiritual Authority

DAVID M. ADAMS

RPP
ROPERPENBERTHY PUBLISHING

Published by RoperPenberthy Publishing Ltd
PO Box 545, Horsham, RH12 4QW

Text copyright David M. Adams 2001

First Published 2001

ISBN 1 903905 07 9

Printed in the United Kingdom.

DEDICATION

These notes were prepared for use in teaching in the Bible School of 'Word of Faith Church', Kiev, Ukraine. I dedicate them to Pastor Sunday Adelaja, who is both an inspiration and an example to me.

CONTENTS

PREFACE

Authority is a key issue in the victorious Christian life. The word 'authority' occurs in NT almost as often as 'love' yet, in comparison, remarkably little is written and taught about authority. Perhaps the spirit of the age has convinced many that authority is the converse of freedom, something heavy and repressive, even in the church. It is not, or at least it shouldn't be. The greatest single influence on my thinking on this topic has been *Spiritual Authority* by Watchman Nee (Christian Fellowship Publishers, New York 1972), which I acknowledge gratefully.

David M. Adams
Leicester, England
January 1997

CHAPTER 1.

Spiritual Authority

Introduction

The reality of existence is that there is a spirit world which controls the physical dimension of space and time in which we live. This spirit world consists of two opposed camps, called kingdoms. There is the kingdom of God (also called the kingdom of heaven), and there is Satan's kingdom. Each kingdom reflects the nature of its head. Satan's kingdom was formed out of a rebellion in heaven against God's authority, and it is opposed to God's values on every point. These two kingdoms are at war with each other, Satan's kingdom being the aggressor.

The issue at stake in this war is one of authority. To whom shall we bow the knee, God or Satan? As Christians, our conflict with Satan is a direct result of our attributing authority to God. The concept of authority is central both to the war with Satan, and to the kingdom of God. This kingdom is being established on earth, as in heaven, so that the world may be renewed along the lines of God's original purpose. Eden-like life shall become a reality on earth, with Christ ruling as King, accompanied in glory by those believers who have overcome the Evil One by their obedience to Jesus as Lord. The work of the kingdom is opposed by Satan, but God has given authority to the Church so that she may enforce the victory Christ won over Satan at Calvary.

In the New Testament (NT) the word 'authority' occurs almost as often as the word 'love' but, in contrast to love, remarkably little is written and taught about it. The purpose of this book is to offer a concise summary of biblical teaching on the nature of the Church's authority, and that of the individual believer. This understanding is basic to success in spiritual warfare, and is especially apposite in our times when the battle is on for the salvation and allegiance of the cities and nations of the world.

Authority - the first question of theology.
The concept of authority underlies every system of theology because until there is agreement upon which sources of knowledge are to be accepted as true, no system of belief can be erected. Here, immediately, we discover that spiritual warfare rages.

Various sources said to reveal truth include: God (which raises the question of how he communicates with man), the Bible, tradition, the church, reason, conscience, and personal experience. According to the relative weight given to such factors, different theological positions emerge.

In the early church there was almost complete agreement that the scriptures are the primary source of revelation. However, as the years passed, there was an increasing tendency to attribute authority also to church tradition. This grew to the extent that by the fourth century tradition had assumed an authority at least equal to that of scripture. This was the situation addressed by the

Reformation (16th century), which rejected this duality of authority, maintaining that all authority is based upon the scriptures, and only the scriptures (Latin: *sola scriptura*).

In responding to the Reformers, the Catholic church further entrenched its position, adding to its insistence on the authority of tradition, the church, and church law, eventually asserting also that the Pope's *ex-cathedra* statements (i.e. when speaking officially) on faith and practice are infallible (1870).

An altogether different emphasis emerged in the 19th century in the form of Protestant liberal theology, which laid emphasis upon man's own reason and subjective experience as the source of authority, the nadir of its achievements being the 20th century 'death of God' theology. These movements accelerated the decline of the western church, especially during the decade of the 1960's.

This book is based upon the traditional evangelical Protestant understanding that all authority originates in God, and that the Bible is the sole, sufficient and complete revelation of his will.

The meaning of the word 'authority'.

The word 'authority' means "legal power or right". In biblical usage it refers to God's absolute right to act as he chooses. In the Old Testament(OT) there are few explicit references to the word 'authority', although the concept is pervasive, and the principles by which God intends authority to be exercised are clearly revealed through a number of dramatic events. In contrast, in the NT, the word 'authority' (Greek: *exousia*) is used no less than 103 times. When compared with the occurrences of *agape* (love, 116), *phileo* (love, tender affection, 26), *dunamis* (power, 123), and *pistis* (faith, 244), it is clear that authority is a key issue for Christians and, moreover, one that is insufficiently taught today.

Exousia has the root meaning "it is lawful", but it is actually used to cover a range of related applications, as is indicated by its translation variously as: authority, liberty, right, strength, power, control, ability, disposal, to be in charge of, and jurisdiction - the sphere of influence in which authority is exercised.

Authority is useless without the power to enforce it, but the distinction between 'power' and 'authority' is finely drawn and often ignored. Fulfilment of God's will is the purpose for which his delegated authority is to be used. Power is the ability to implement will; it is authority in action. The effectiveness of a policeman on traffic duty lies in his authority, which is backed by the power of the law.

Authority : legal power or right.
Will : the purpose for which authority is to be used
Power : the ability to implement will. Authority in action.

God works by the exercise of authority. His will is an expression of his authority, and his power is that authority in action. He has delegated authority to the Church so that she may co-operate with him in establishing the kingdom on earth, but she is able to exercise that authority effectively only insofar as she knows the will of God.

Your kingdom come, your will be done on earth as it is in heaven. (Matthew 6:10)

All authority belongs to God.
The Bible states clearly that all authority belongs to and derives from God.

The earth is the Lord's, and everything in it, the world and all who live in it. (Psalm 24:1)

The Lord has established his throne in heaven, and his kingdom rules over all. (Psalm 103:19)

Yours [Father] is the kingdom and the power and the glory forever. (Matthew 6:13)

A man can receive only what is given him from heaven. (John 3:27)

There is no authority except from God. (Romans 13:1 RSV)

Within the Trinity, the Father is distinguished from the Son and the Holy Spirit by his role. Although all three Persons of the Trinity are equal in importance, personhood, deity, and power, the Father has a leadership role which requires greater authority. This authority is now vested in Jesus. About 540 BC, in an awesome vision, Daniel saw:

> *one like a son of man, coming with the clouds of heaven. He approached the Ancient of Days and was led into his presence. He was given authority, glory and sovereign power; all peoples, nations and men of every language worshipped him. His dominion is an everlasting dominion that will not pass away, and his kingdom is one that will never be destroyed.*
> *(Daniel 7:14)*

After his resurrection Jesus confirmed to his followers that *all authority in heaven and earth has been given to me (Matthew 28:18)*; and that he holds the *keys of death and Hades (Revelation 1:18)*. This authority he will exercise until the end comes, when he will hand over

> *the kingdom to God the Father after he has destroyed all dominion, authority and power. For he must reign until he has put all his enemies under his feet. (1 Corinthians 15:24)*

The reason for the Church's authority.

Thus, the purpose for which all authority is vested in Jesus is the kingdom, which God is establishing on earth, as in heaven. By definition, the kingdom of heaven is that realm within which his rule and authority are established. God's plan is to re-establish on earth a kingdom characterised by Eden-like life, and he is doing this by and through the Church. Jesus delegates his authority to the

Church so that the work of bringing in his kingdom on earth may be completed. This is the context in which all authority is to be understood and exercised.

Why is authority so important? Because God's work is done primarily through the exercise of authority, rather than by power, which is his authority in action. The war against Satan is not so much a power struggle as a truth encounter, God's truth against Satan's lies.

God's work is done primarily through the exercise of authority, rather than by power, which is his authority in action.

Obedience to God's will or rebellion?

Authority cannot exist in a vacuum. The exercise of authority implies a response on behalf of those living under it. That response can be either obedience or rebellion. God's authority represents himself, and his will is an expression of his authority. Thus, to rebel

God's authority represents himself, and his will is an expression of his authority.

against his authority is to rebel against God himself. Sin is but the consequence of that rebellion. Therefore, rebellion is more fundamental than sin against God's holiness, because it is a reflection of a heart attitude which substitutes obedience to Satan for obedience to God. In other words, it substitutes death for life, and that God cannot allow, because his will is expressed in words which themselves are life. Therefore, in scripture God repeatedly emphasises the value he places upon strict obedience to his word, and disobedience carries fearsome consequences.

Satan is sometimes claimed to have been an archangel who rebelled against God's authority, and was ejected from heaven as a result, although nowhere in scripture is this stated explicitly. The claim rests upon a disputed interpretation of *Isaiah 14:13-14.* However, we are on firmer ground with *Jude (v6 RSV)* who refers to *angels that did not keep their own position but left their proper dwelling,* and *2 Peter 2:4* which states that *God did not spare angels when they sinned, but sent them to hell.* The principle remains, however, that rebellion against God always results in judgement. King Saul was more concerned with his own standing and image than with obedience to God's word through the prophet Samuel. He lost his kingdom in consequence.

> *But Samuel replied: "Does the LORD delight in burnt offerings and sacrifices as much as in obeying the voice of the LORD? To obey is better than sacrifice, and to heed is better than the fat of rams. For rebellion is like the sin of divination, and arrogance like the evil of idolatry. Because you have rejected the word of the LORD, he has rejected you as king." (1 Samuel 15:22-23)*

CHAPTER 2.

How and Why Authority was Established.

How authority on earth was lost.

In the beginning God created two kinds of being: angels, spirit beings to live with him in eternity; and man, to live in the world of time and space. To man he gave authority over everything on earth *(Genesis 1:28-30)*. However, God foresaw that there would be rebellion amongst both populations, thereby challenging his authority and incurring his wrath.

There was war in heaven, with Satan and his followers being ejected. In a parallel scenario on earth, Adam and Eve chose to fall for the devil's deception. In choosing to believe in Satan rather than God, Adam submitted to Satan and thereby placed himself under Satan's authority. Like Satan, he too was ejected from his relationship of intimacy with God *(Genesis 3:24)*. God was also affected in that he lost in Adam the channel through which his authority was intended to flow in his kingdom on earth. How was this sin to be atoned for and God's authority re-established on earth, such that Satan would no longer have authority over God's people? **How authority on earth was re-established.**

The understanding we now seek lies at the very limits of what is revealed in scripture. The concept of deity implies a being vastly greater than ourselves, in intelligence, power, and every other aspect of his nature. Inevitably, then, on all sides our understanding runs out into the mystery of God. We place important-sounding labels on these boundaries, words such as 'Trinity', 'eternity', 'atonement', 'incarnation', 'resurrection' and 'ascension', but they serve mainly to describe our ignorance. We also face awesome mystery as we attempt to see how kingdom authority was re-established on earth, and what that cost.

No created man could possibly appease a Holy God, or re-establish obedience on earth. Therefore, within the Trinity it was agreed that the Son would come to earth as a created being, in order to show that it is possible to live a life of perfect obedience and submission to the Father, regardless of the worst Satan could do to prevent that. Through his sinless life, the shedding of his blood, and his undeserved death on a cross, he would become the final, all-sufficient, all-atoning sacrifice for the sins of all mankind. By his perfect obedience as a man, and his steadfast refusal of every temptation that is common to man, he would re-establish God's kingdom authority on earth, and win forgiveness of sins and eternal life for all who received and believed in him. This is an awesome mystery, but let us probe deeper. The key scripture here is *Philippians 2:6-11.* Christ Jesus,

who being in very nature God, did not consider equality with God something to be grasped, but made himself nothing, taking the very nature of a servant, being made in human likeness.

From this we see that Jesus humbled himself first in heaven, laying aside his glory, in order to be born as a man. Thus, he bound himself to live a life of perfect submission to the Father's will, knowing that this was the only way he could return to heaven and see the Father's will for his creation fulfilled. If he failed through rebellion on even the smallest issue, all would be lost. Charles Wesley (1707-88) understood this well:

> Let earth and heaven combine
> Angels and men agree
> To praise in songs divine
> The incarnate Deity
> Our God contracted to a span
> Incomprehensibly made man
>
> He laid His glory by
> Hewrapped him in our clay
> Unmarked by human eye
> The latent godhead lay
> Infant of days he here became
> And bore the mild Immanuel's name

The Father loves the Son and has placed everything in his hands. (John 3:35)

Christ's victory over Satan.

The reason the Son of God appeared was to destroy the devil's work (1 John 3:8). In this he was totally victorious, in (1) his life, (2) his death, and (3) in his exaltation. Through the completeness of this victory, God's objective was attained and his kingdom re-established on earth.

(1) Christ's victory in his personal life. Remarkably, as a man Jesus had to learn obedience. Thus: *Although he was a son, he learned obedience from what he suffered and, once made perfect, he became the source of eternal salvation for all who obey him (Hebrews 5:8-9).* The perfection spoken of here implies that the process of learning through suffering made him complete in human experience, not that he was in any way imperfect and needed correction. The thing for us to appreciate is that Jesus did not come to earth already full of obedience: that would have made him more than fully human.

No, he shared our life in every way. Therefore, like any and every human child, he had to *learn* obedience the hard way, through suffering.

Immediately after his baptism in the Jordan river, Jesus was led by the Spirit to a desert place where he was tempted by Satan *(Luke 4:1-12)*. The three temptations were to body (lust of the flesh, *v2-4*), soul (lust of the eyes, *v5-8*), and spirit (pride of life, *v9-12*). Each was resisted using a word of God from scripture. In this, as throughout his life, he was sinless *(Hebrews 4:15)*. This victory in his personal life opened the way for:

(2) Christ's victory on the cross, which was on behalf of all mankind and, thus, is often called his 'representative' victory. *Philippians 2:8* shows that *as a man* he again humbled himself before the Father, obediently going to the cross, having proved that it is possible for a man to live in total obedience to God.

And being found in appearance as a man, he humbled himself and became
obedient to death— even death on a cross!
(Philippians 2:8)

The writers of the NT epistles are clear, that it was at the cross that Satan was decisively defeated.

Since the children have flesh and blood, he too shared in their
humanity so that by his death he might destroy him who holds the
power of death—that is, the devil. (Hebrews 2:14)

And having disarmed the powers and authorities, he made a public
spectacle of them, triumphing over them by the cross. (Colossians
2:15)

(3) Christ's victory in heavenly realms. His resurrection and ascension declared his victory also in heavenly places. He has totally demolished every vestige of Satan's rule.

Because of Jesus' total victory, the Father exalted him *as a man* to the highest place of honour in heaven, and conferred on him the title and authority of 'Lord'. This title did not exist before his exaltation. It was his reward from the Father for his life of perfect submission and obedience *as a man*. The word 'Lord' (Greek: *kurios*) derives from a root meaning 'supreme in authority'.

> *Therefore God exalted him to the highest place and gave him the name that is above every name, that at the name of Jesus every knee should bow, in heaven and on earth and under the earth, and every tongue confess that Jesus Christ is Lord, to the glory of God the Father. (Philippians 2:9-11)*

> *Therefore let all Israel be assured of this: God has made this Jesus, whom you crucified, both Lord and Christ. (Acts 2:36)*

Thus, after his exaltation Jesus was able to say: ***All** authority in heaven and on earth has been given to me. (Matthew 28:18)*. Everything in heaven and on earth is subject to him: *he is head over every power and authority (Colossians 2:10)*. God the Father has:

> *raised him from the dead and seated him at his right hand in the heavenly realms, far above all rule and authority, power and dominion, and every title that can be given, not only in the present age but also in the one to come. And God placed all things under his feet and appointed him to be head over everything for the church, which is his body, the fullness of him who fills everything in every way. (Ephesians 1:20-23)*

As a man, Jesus had authority over all the works of the Evil One. Like the first Adam, Jesus, the last Adam, received authority from God. Unlike the first Adam, he didn't lose it because he lived a sinless life, perfect in obedience, allowing the devil no foothold. Through Jesus' obedience *as a man* our salvation became possible. If he had rebelled against the Father's authority in even the smallest matter, all mankind would have been doomed to death. This is the man who taught that even to *dwell* upon a malicious or lustful thought was to commit the sin. Imagine the lifelong self-control that implies - and still it was said of him that he was the most joyful of men (*Hebrews 1:9*)!

For just as through the disobedience of the one man the many were made sinners, so also through the obedience of the one man the many will be made righteous. (Romans 5:19)

Love is the reason.

Every parent can begin to identify with Abraham in his heart-rending decision to obey God and sacrifice His only son, Isaac (*Genesis 22*). We can follow with him on the journey to the place of sacrifice, and imagine the long-drawn-out agony of heart and mind that was his. But all heaven and earth must stand in awe at that which God, through Jesus, did for all mankind.

For God so loved the world that he gave his one and only son, that whoever believes in him shall not perish but have eternal life. (John 3:16)

The authority thereby re-established on earth is precious, awesome, and holy. It is now entrusted to the church so that the kingdom may be established on earth. What, then, is this kingdom for which the Son of God humbled himself twice over, this kingdom over which angels and demons join battle in response to the prayers and commands of mere mortals, even of children?

Why authority was re-established on earth: the kingdom.[1,2]

The kingdom was the primary topic of Jesus' preaching. It has a three-fold time structure: (1) Jesus' earthly ministry; (2) the age of the church (i.e. from his exaltation to his return); (3) the period following his return to earth. Jesus himself is the kingdom in person, because he is totally submitted to the Father's will.

The Greek word *basileia* is usually translated as 'kingdom', but it can also "have the dynamic meaning of 'rule', 'reign', 'kingship', as well as the concrete meaning of 'realm', or 'territory governed by a king'." Although the phrase 'the kingdom of God' is absent from OT, the concept of God as king, and of his kingly rule, pervades it. He is a covenant-making God, and the covenants are the constitution of his kingdom.

It is important to grasp that the kingdom Jesus preached "is not an ideal moral order, nor is it more or less equivalent with divine sovereignty. Rather it answers to the great OT expectation", the "realisation of Israel's hope, the fulfilment of the covenant promises made to the fathers"[1]. It is that which must come to pass before there can be a new heaven and a new earth. It is God's will for planet earth, and it shall be. But what is the relationship of the kingdom to the church? In the Bible,

> "the kingdom is not identified with its subjects. They are the people of God's rule who enter it, live under it, and are governed by it. The church is the community of the Kingdom, but never the Kingdom itself. Jesus' disciples belong to the Kingdom as the Kingdom belongs to them; but they are not the Kingdom. The Kingdom is the rule of God; the church is the society of men."[2]

"The kingdom is the rule of God; the church is the society of men."

Luke records Jesus as saying that:

> *"The kingdom of God does not come visibly, nor will people say, 'Here it is', or 'There it is', because the kingdom of God is within you."(Luke 17:20-21 NIV)*

This teaching is problematical in that the Greek uses the word *entos*, which may be translated either as 'among' or 'within'. In that Jesus stood there physically in the crowd, fully submitted to the Father's will, it was true to say that *the kingdom of God is among you*, and indeed this is the generally preferred translation of this passage. However, since the kingdom is a matter of a heart attitude of submission to the Father, not visible to the eye, the kingdom may also be said to be *within* us, as well as among us, the church.

> *I declare to you, brothers, that flesh and blood cannot inherit the kingdom of God, nor does the perishable inherit the imperishable. (1 Corinthians 15:50)*

Called to obedience to Jesus Christ.
God's kingdom thus begins with Jesus, but it includes those

who are the church. Our call as Christians is to co-operate with God in bringing in his kingdom, *on earth as in heaven*. As disciples (pupils, learners) we are to know God's will and choose to obey it: that is, we are to be consciously submitted to his authority in all things. Paul prefaced *Philippians 2:6-11* with these words: *Your attitude should be the same as that of Christ Jesus.* Jesus, as a man, *learned obedience from what he suffered (Hebrews 5:8).* So must we, but note that it is not the suffering which counts, as much as the obedience we learn through it.

> *The world must learn that I love the Father and that I do exactly what my Father has commanded me. (John 14:31)*

> *I have come to do your will, O God. (Hebrews 10:7)*

> *"Abba, Father," he said, "everything is possible for you. Take this cup from me. Yet not what I will, but what you will." (Mark 14:36)*

The obedience expected, which should be the fruit of our love for him and not simply the product of dead legalism, is clearly specified in scripture:

> *Do you not know that the wicked will not inherit the kingdom of God? Do not be deceived: Neither the sexually immoral nor idolaters nor adulterers nor male prostitutes nor homosexual offenders nor thieves nor the greedy nor drunkards nor slanderers nor swindlers will inherit the kingdom of God. And that is what some of you were. But you were washed, you were sanctified, you were justified in the name of the Lord Jesus Christ and by the Spirit of our God. (1 Corinthians 6:9-11)*

The church, the community of the kingdom, is destined to become the Bride of Christ and, finally, the Holy City. It is the community of those who have chosen to walk in obedience to Christ because of their love for him.

> *"Blessed are those who wash their robes, that they may have the right to the tree of life and may go through the gates into the city. Outside are the dogs, those who practice magic arts, the sexually*

immoral, the murderers, the idolaters and everyone who loves and practices falsehood. *(Revelation 22:14-15)*

Obedience to God results in *righteousness, peace and joy in the Holy Spirit (Romans 14:17)*. Moreover, since action in obedience to the Father's will opens the way for manifestation of his power, it follows that *the kingdom of God is not a matter of talk but of power (1 Corinthians 4:20)* as, indeed, Jesus stated: *If I drive out demons by the finger of God, then the kingdom of God has come to you. (Luke 11:20)* Therefore:

> *We have been chosen according to the foreknowledge of God the Father, by the sanctifying work of the Spirit, for obedience to Jesus Christ and sprinkling by his blood. (1 Peter 1:2)*

> *Through him and for his name's sake, we received grace and apostleship to call people from among all the Gentiles to the obedience that comes from faith. (Romans 1:5)*

> *Keeping God's commands is what counts. (1 Corinthians 7:19)*

> *We take captive every thought to make it obedient to Christ. (2 Corinthians 10:5)*

As Christians our call is to obey God, and thereby to fulfil our pre-ordained kingdom function and purpose, remembering that the Father has vested all authority in Christ *in order to* establish the kingdom on earth. Our call is to obedience, not to self-denial. Self-denial is but the consequence of choosing to obey. Jesus said:

> *"If you want to enter life, obey the commandments." (Matthew 19:17)*

> *"... teaching them to obey everything I have commanded you." (Matthew 28:20)*

> *"Blessed rather are those who hear the word of God and obey it." (Luke 11:28)*

"If anyone loves me, he will obey my teaching." (John 14:23)

"Do whatever he tells you." (John 2:5)

CHAPTER **3**.

*How God's delegated
authority works.*

The need to be under delegated authority.

As Christians we have been chosen by God for obedience to Jesus Christ (*1 Peter 1:2*). The first and greatest commandment is to *love the Lord your God with all your heart and with all your soul and with all your mind and with all your strength (Mark 12:30)*. In keeping this commandment we show our love for God by our obedience, for obedience is the proof of our love (*John 14:23*), and the demonstration of being submitted to his authority. In this we are directly answerable to God himself.

However, God's kingdom is so structured that everyone is expected to be under delegated authority. It is the principle by which the body of Christ, the church, to whom Christ has delegated his authority, operates. Unless a believer is co-ordinated into the local church and under authority within it, he cannot be effective by God's standards. There is no place for the loner in God's economy. Therefore we are required also to submit to authority within the church.

The authority the Lord gave me [is] for building you up, not for tearing you down (2 Corinthians 13:10)

God has ordained levels of authority in the body. In an individual church there will generally be 'elders', 'deacons' (the labels may vary), and probably others under them, all being subject to the overall authority of the Pastor. In turn, the Pastor will (or should) be subject either to others in the hierarchy of his organisation, or to apostles. Every Christian should know whose delegated authority he comes under.

Obey your leaders and submit to their authority. They keep watch over you as men who must give an account. Obey them so that their work will be a joy, not a burden, for that would be of no advantage to you. (Hebrews 13:17)

Now we ask you, brothers, to respect those who work hard among you, who are over you in the Lord and who admonish you. Hold them in the highest regard in love because of their work. Live in peace with each other. (1 Thessalonians 5:12-13)

The elders who direct the affairs of the church well are worthy of double honour, especially those whose work is preaching and teaching. (1 Timothy 5:17)

Thus, every believer must have his or her own intimate, personal relationship with Jesus, and in that respect is under his direct authority. Nevertheless, in operational terms, the kingdom of God works by means of delegated authority and every citizen of it is to find his appointed place of submission within it.

God delegates authority to man, but man himself must obey both God's authority and the authority of those set over him.

Many in the church today regard themselves as subject only to God's authority, answerable directly to him. They float from church to church but never settle in any. Unwilling to work or accept responsibility, they often claim sweetly to be "doing what God tells me". They are of little use in the kingdom. They will never achieve their potential in Christ, and can be a distraction and a burden to the church. The church is God's instrument for establishing the kingdom. Therefore, as in any organisation charged with a specific aim and mission, each person must know whose authority they are under, and whom they are to obey. Why? Basically, for two reasons.

The purpose of being under authority in the church.

1. Blessing and training. Submission to authority is the entrance to many of God's blessings. One crucial way this happens is by those who are more mature in the faith being placed over newer Christians, in order to disciple them. Indeed, this is a function of being under authority all the way up the chain of command. By this means, God's riches are made available to us more readily than if we had had to struggle for them ourselves. We can take advantage of the spiritual wisdom and experience of others, thereby growing to maturity more quickly than otherwise. This is not to suggest that God brings us to maturity only by this means, but there is no doubt that new Christians who are actively taught and discipled do grow more quickly and more fruitfully than those who are not.

Moreover, it is in the early stages that the believer starts to develop a servant heart himself, as he begins with small things. Most churches find that more are willing to preach than to clean toilets! This is doubly disturbing, because it shows (1) absence of a servant heart; (2) a desire to offer opinions and to be seen, rather than to tremble at God's word.

Delegated authority is God's licence to move into a wider sphere of service, and it is not given to those who are unwilling to do the menial and often unseen practical jobs of service. You cannot choose your point of entry on God's ladder of service. God entrusts his delegated authority only to those who have proved themselves willing to submit to the authority of others, in the church and in the world.

2. Active service. The church is not just an association of people with a common interest, neither is it a hospital - it is primarily a barracks. The church is working towards a phenomenal future as the New Jerusalem, but to get there she must first engage in warfare under her Commander, the Lord of Hosts. This military mind-set, if adopted generally by the church, would transform attitudes to authority. If the church operates as a well-disciplined army, the work of the kingdom in all its urgency, richness and variety will get done efficiently, but not if it's an undisciplined rabble.

Principles of living under delegated authority.

1.   The first principle of kingdom authority (above) is that the believer is to obey both God and the delegated authority under which God has placed him.

2.   The second principle is: that a man in authority is to be respected, not because of what he is in himself, but because of the godly authority and anointing he bears. He has been chosen to represent God in that situation. Therefore, to rebel against God's delegated authority is to rebel against God himself.

3.   A man in authority must not defend himself. God will do it for him, because it is God's honour which is at stake.

4.   Rebellion originates in hell. It is contagious, and it causes God's anointing on a work to lift until the matter is resolved. God's judgement is that the rebellious become slaves to those who obey.

> *He who rebels against authority is rebelling against what God has instituted, and those who do so will bring judgement upon themselves. (Romans 13:2)*

5.   The person first placed in a work by God is the one in authority.

6.   Service based upon personal initiative is unacceptable to God. Everyone in God's kingdom is to work under the authority of a leader chosen and anointed by God.

These principles are taught in the OT by means of a variety of dramatic incidents, of which the following are a selection.

Adam and Eve *(Genesis 1:26 to 3:24).*
      Jesus, *the last Adam (1 Corinthians 15:45), learned obedience (Hebrews 5:8).* This was the principle God used with the first Adam: he gave him authority over all created things on earth, but also, in giving him the command *not (to) eat from the tree of the knowledge of good and evil,* placed Adam under his own (God's) authority. Eve, in turn, was placed also under Adam's authority, being required therefore to obey both God and her husband. She chose to act on the basis of her own desire, thereby disobeying Adam and rebelling against God. Adam too was disobedient. Judgement followed, sentence was quickly applied, and they were banned from Eden. From this we learn:

      (1) God delegates authority to man, but man himself must obey God's authority if he is to exercise delegated authority.

      (2) The person first placed in a situation by God is the one in authority. Adam was in authority over Eve. In Israeli families, the firstborn son has special privileges, and likewise, the rule of primogeniture applies in many societies. The man God uses to found a work or a church is the one who has God's authority there.

      (3) To rebel against God's delegated authority is to rebel against God.

Noah and Ham *(Genesis 9:20-27).*
      One of Noah's sons, Ham, happened upon his father lying in a tent naked and in a drunken stupor. He reported this discovery to his older brothers Shem and Japheth who, being men of high

moral character, entered their father's tent walking backwards and dropped a cover over him, averting their eyes meanwhile. Sober again, Noah pieced the story together and reacted by calling down blessings upon the older boys but a curse upon Ham: *"the lowest of slaves will he be to his brothers"*. Although not stated explicitly, it seems that Ham had found his father's lapse cause for amusement and, quite possibly also, of ribaldry. What does this incident teach?

(4) A man in authority is to be respected, not because of who or what he is in himself, but because of the authority of the Lord which he bears. Ham failed to make this distinction, not honouring his father's authority in the home.

(5) Those who refuse to obey authority shall become slaves to those who do obey.

> To him who overcomes, I will give the right to sit with
> me on my throne.... (Revelation 3:21)

> ... and they (the saints) will reign on earth. (Revelation 5:10)

Nadab and Abihu *(Leviticus 10:1-11), and* **King Uzziah** *(2 Chronicles 26:16-21).*

Aaron was the first High Priest in Israel, and his four sons were consecrated to assist him. Two of his sons, Nadab and Abihu, took their censers and *offered unauthorised fire before the Lord, contrary to his command. So fire came out from the presence of the Lord and consumed them, and they died before the Lord.* The account of this incident is followed by a new instruction from God to the effect that priests must not consume alcoholic drinks before ministering to him, the implication being that Nadab and Abihu had been drunk when they transgressed Their God-given function was to serve under Aaron's authority, but they chose to act independently, thinking that a sacrifice would be just as acceptable to God if offered by them rather than at Aaron's instigation. Their presumption led immediately to death.

A similar incident is recorded of King Uzziah of Judah (767-

742 BC). In the early years of his reign he sought the Lord and God gave him success. Having become very powerful, in arrogance he entered the temple one day intending to burn incense at the golden altar, ignoring the anxious and courageous pleas of the priests who reminded him that such service to God was the preserve of Levites sanctified for that purpose. Instantly, God afflicted him with leprosy. He remained a leper, living out his life in isolation, whilst his son Jotham ruled in his stead. Our lesson?

(6) God does not accept service offered on the basis of personal initiative. Everyone in his kingdom must work under the authority of a leader chosen and anointed by God. Ministry is ordained in heaven, and not on earth in the mind of man.

Aaron and Miriam *(Numbers 12:1-15).*

Moses had married a gentile, contrary to God's will. As his elder brother and sister, Aaron and Miriam had every right to reprimand him, and did so. What they had not understood was that although Moses was indeed their little brother, God had placed him in authority over all Israel, and therefore over them also. Later, Jesus' brothers were to have a similar problem. God's judgement on Miriam (who presumably led Aaron in this incident) was to afflict her with leprosy for a week. During that time, the pillar of cloud, signifying the presence of God, was lifted and Israel could not travel. Conclusions?

(7) Rebellion amongst God's people causes his anointing on the work to leave until the issue is resolved.

(8) A man whom God has placed in authority need not defend himself: God will do it for him.

Moses *was more humble than anyone else on the face of the earth.* For that reason he was able to handle God's delegated authority, for he was himself already subject to God's authority. He was secure in his relationship with God, and in his anointing for leadership, a position he had not sought and, indeed, had resisted *(Exodus 4:13).* Authority is given by God to whom he chooses, and that authority is resisted at the peril of those who rebel.

Korah's rebellion *(Numbers 16).*

Each of the above incidents has shown something of the fearsome consequences of rebellion against God-given authority. The next, like that of Adam and Eve, nakedly reveals the truly hellish origin of all rebellion.

Korah led over 250 Levites in a challenge to Moses' authority. *They became insolent and rose up against Moses. They came as a group to oppose Moses and Aaron.* Moses' response is a classic of spiritual warfare: he reacted by coming against them in the opposite spirit. Thus, he fell on his face before God, seeking his wisdom for the moment.

This rebellion mirrored that of Satan in heaven. The Levites were the priestly tribe, chosen by God to serve him. Korah was from the Kohathite clan, and their specific duty was to carry the most holy parts of the tabernacle furniture when camp was moved. After the priests, they were the Levites chosen to be closest to God's presence. But now, Moses said to them, *you are trying to get the priesthood too. It is against the Lord that you and all your followers have banded together. Who is Aaron that you should grumble against him?*

The rebellion spread still further but was concluded when God acted: *The earth opened its mouth and swallowed them, with their households and all Korah's men and all their possessions.* They went down alive into the grave, with everything they owned. The lessons?

(9) Rebellion originates in hell. It was said of Korah's people that *these men have treated the Lord with contempt.* Elsewhere in scripture, any who despise the word of the Lord are dealt with severely. Rebellion is contagious. It spreads like an infectious disease.

David and Saul.

The story of David's relationship with King Saul illustrates a further principle. God had rejected Saul as king because of his disobedience (*1 Samuel 15*), although he was allowed to continue for a while in that office. Meanwhile, God had sent the prophet Samuel to anoint the young David as King in succession to Saul. Soon afterwards David entered Saul's service, rapidly achieving national fame by killing the Philistine giant Goliath. David's subsequent military successes in Saul's army soon eclipsed those of Saul himself. Jealousy set in, and before long Saul was hunting David, intent on murdering him.

David had two opportunities to kill Saul but refused to harm him because of the anointing upon the King. In one of these incidents, David cut off a piece of Saul's robe as Saul relieved himself in a cave, to prove that Saul had been at his mercy, but was immediately distressed at what he had done.

> *Afterward, David was conscience-stricken for having cut off a corner of his robe. He said to his men, "The LORD forbid that I should do such a thing to my master, the Lord's anointed, or lift my hand against him; for he is the anointed of the LORD." (1 Samuel 24:5-6)*

Later, Saul was mortally wounded in battle and, with the enemy closing in on him, instructed a young man to finish him off. When the young man reported to David what he had done to ease the King's last moments, expecting a reward:

> *David asked him, "Why were you not afraid to lift your hand to destroy the Lord's anointed?" Then David called one of his men and said, "Go, strike him down!" So he struck him down, and he died. For David had said to him, "Your blood be on your own head. Your own mouth testified against you when you said, 'I killed the Lord's anointed.'" (2 Samuel 1:14-16)*

(10) In being subject to a man in authority, we are not being subject to him as a person, but to God's anointing which is on him.

The anointing which God gives a person is holy, separating him to God for that work. Therefore, to interfere with that which is holy carries severe penalties. In respecting the anointing which was upon Saul, David was obedient to God's authority exercised through the King, even though the King was corrupt. Therefore God could trust David with great authority, because David's heart was submitted to God's authority.

Jesus taught that to hate one's brother is akin to murder. To harbour such thoughts is a dangerous spiritually as the act of murder.

We conclude:
God's kingdom is established and extended by the exercise of his authority. Indeed, the kingdom is the reason the authority is given in the first place. Thus, rebellion strikes at the very root of what God is doing in this world. It challenges him and his intentions directly, and therefore cannot be tolerated.

CHAPTER 4.

The Authority of Jesus and of the Church.

Jesus' authority.

Authority was a keynote of Jesus' ministry. The people saw that *he taught as one who had authority, and not as their teachers of the law (Matthew 7:29).* Indeed, *they were amazed at his teaching, because his message had authority (Luke 4:32).*

The first signs of this gift are seen in his tutorial in the Jerusalem temple at age 12 *(Luke 2:46-47).* Here was this pre-adolescent Galilean country boy, able to cut through all the obfuscation of the rabbinical teaching of his day, ask penetrating questions from unusual angles, and give answers of a quality and content which the teachers themselves envied. Fanciful? Every university teacher knows that just occasionally a student appears who has exceptional clarity and precision of mind and thought: here was one such. Why was he not identified and sought out for early training in the Jerusalem law school? Of course, such was not the Father's will, but even so, some of the teachers must have felt threatened even then by this first contact with such a crisp and original mind.

There is an almost tangible air of authority about Jesus as the wedding drama at Cana unfolds. *Do whatever he tells you* his mother told the servants (*John 2:5*). Having seen him heal a paralysed man and assure him that his sins were forgiven, *the crowd were filled with awe; and they praised God, who had given such authority to men (Matthew 9:8)*. As his ministry unfolded, at a word demons left those they had infected, the lame walked, the blind saw, and lives were transformed by the authoritative assurance of sins forgiven. Even the disturbed religious leaders enquired: *Who gave you this authority? (Matthew 21:23)*.

It was left to a Roman soldier to formulate most clearly what was happening. He knew what it was like to be part of a chain of command. When he saw Jesus operating in the same relaxed and confident authority as did his senior officers, he knew that only a word from him was needed to heal the servant whose need had brought him to Jesus (*Matthew 8:5-13*).

Jesus spelled out the extent of his own authority while on earth. Insofar as his own life was concerned, *he had authority to lay it down and authority to take it up again (John 10:18)*. With respect to the world, his authority included *all people (John 17:2)*. Specifically, he had authority: (1) to teach (*Matthew 7:29; Mark 1:22*); (2) to forgive sins (*Matthew 9:6; Mark 2:10; Luke 5:24*); (3) to judge (*John 5:27*); (4) to give eternal life (*John 17:2*); and (5) to heal and deliver, the latter including authority to raise the dead by delivering them from the power of death (*Matthew 10:1; Mark 1:27, 3:15, 6:7; Luke 4:36, 9:1*). However, there were limits even to his authority whilst on earth:

Jesus said to them, "You will indeed drink from my cup, but to sit at my right or left is not for me to grant. These places belong to those for whom they have been prepared by my Father." (Matthew 20:23)

"No one knows about that day or hour, not even the angels in heaven, nor the Son, but only the Father. (Matthew 24:36)

We now review how his delegated authority is to work on earth until he returns.

God-given authority relationships.

God's will is that his kingdom, and world society, are structured in a clear chain of command manner, within the following categories. In this Chapter we review the first of these.

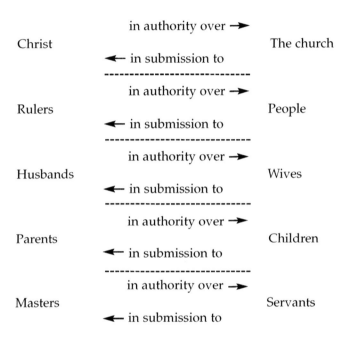

	in authority over →	
Christ		The church
	← in submission to	
	in authority over →	
Rulers		People
	← in submission to	
	in authority over →	
Husbands		Wives
	← in submission to	
	in authority over →	
Parents		Children
	← in submission to	
	in authority over →	
Masters		Servants
	← in submission to	

The church's authority.

Of the above categories, the Church is unique in that Christ is not just in authority over her: she is his body, and he is her head. In this intimate spiritual union, the head is committed to bringing the Church into perfection, so that she may be *without stain or wrinkle or any other blemish, but holy and blameless (Ephesians 5:27)*. In the other four categories both authority and submission are likely to be imperfect, but the Church is the platform on which God can and will demonstrate his kingdom life in all its perfection

Given Jesus' prophetic statement that anyone with faith in him would do greater things than he (*John 14:12*), it follows that the delegated authority of both the individual believer and of the church must be similarly all-encompassing although, plainly, only God can forgive sins and give eternal life.

Authority to make disciples.

Thus, Jesus' authority over all people is mirrored in his direction to the church to make disciples of all nations (*Matthew 28:19*); she is assured that success will attend her efforts:

> *After this I looked and there before me was a great multitude that no one could count, from every nation, tribe, people and language, standing before the throne and in front of the Lamb. ...... And they cried out in a loud voice: "Salvation belongs to our God, who sits on the throne, and to the Lamb." (Revelation 7:9-10)*

(1) To make disciples means to teach those who have been brought into the church, so that they may grow up into maturity in the faith. Teaching is one of the five-fold ministries (*Ephesians 4:11-13; Romans 12:7*). The church therefore has God's authority to teach. Indeed, the apostles are insistent that the church must not only teach but must also keep her doctrines pure (e.g. *Encourage others by sound doctrine and refute those who oppose it (Titus 1:9)*). The word 'doctrine' is simply an anglicised form of the Greek word for 'teaching'.

Allied to teaching is the authority for building up and encouraging each other (*2 Corinthians 10:8, 13:10*). Even in matters of discipline within the church, the aim is always redemptive, to build up rather than to pull down.

> *Encourage and rebuke with all authority. (Titus 2:15)*

> *Therefore encourage one another and build each other up, just as in fact you are doing. (1 Thessalonians 5:11)*

> *But encourage one another daily, as long as it is called Today, so*

that none of you may be hardened by sin's deceitfulness. (Hebrews 3:13)

Authority to forgive sins.

In respect of (2) (3) & (4) (above), only God can forgive sins and give eternal life, but Jesus specifically authorised his disciples to assure those whom they judged to be truly penitent, that they had Christ's forgiveness.

And with that he breathed on them and said, "Receive the Holy Spirit. If you forgive anyone his sins, they are forgiven; if you do not forgive them, they are not forgiven." (John 20:22-23)

"The principle is clear. To the Church as the fellowship of the Spirit is given the authority of Christ himself as Pardoner and Judge. But only so far as the Church in and through its members fulfils the condition - *receive the Holy Spirit* - can it discharge this function" (William Temple)[1]. It is not the power to forgive sins that is hereby entrusted to the church, but the power to proclaim that forgiveness.

Then David said to Nathan, "I have sinned against the LORD." Nathan replied, "The LORD has taken away your sin. You are not going to die." (2 Samuel 12:13)

Authority over all the works of the devil.

(5) The church's power over the Evil One is comprehensive. Mark records (*16:15-18*) that after his resurrection, Jesus commissioned the church to begin the work of world evangelisation but, unlike Matthew and Luke, adds:

And these signs will accompany those who believe: In my name they will drive out demons; they will speak in new tongues; they will pick up snakes with their hands; and when they drink deadly poison, it will not hurt them at all; they will place their hands on sick people, and they will get well."

In this, Jesus confirms and elaborates authority previously and variously given to the apostles and the seventy two, and never cancelled.

> *He called his twelve disciples to him and gave them authority to drive out evil spirits and to heal every disease and sickness. (Matthew 10:1)*

> *I have given you authority to trample on snakes and scorpions and to overcome all the power of the enemy; nothing will harm you. (Luke 10:19)*

Once the church in our time wakes up to the implications of this authority, it will be unstoppable. Its not power that gets the results, but authority.

David Hathaway (Director of Eurovision), who is currently seeing awesome evangelistic and healing results in his ministry in Russia and Ukraine writes[2]:

"So many sense, correctly, the need for power in healing, knowing that the power is through the baptism and anointing of the Holy Spirit. Then I see and hear them shouting, supposedly to demonstrate the power - or more often praying long prayers in tongues. But we have **authority** over demons and sickness!"

"In the natural order of command in the world, those with real authority don't shout. Usually, those who do shout don't have the authority! Look at the scripture. It says in *Matthew 8:16: He cast out spirits with his WORD, and healed all who were sick.* I believe that although I have had a ministry of healing throughout my life, it is only since finding this authority that the present anointing has come."

Its not power that gets the results, but authority.

The keys of the kingdom.[3]
The church was and is being raised by God to co-operate with him in bringing in the kingdom. In the broadest sense, therefore, her work is spiritual warfare, and that warfare has a two-fold aspect. (1) She is to "plunder hell to populate heaven" (R.

Bonnke), and (2) she is to keep her own house in order meanwhile. The authority to do these things was conferred graphically by Jesus (*Matthew 16:18-19*) using the metaphor of 'keys', in words which his disciples would have recognised as fulfilling the messianic precedent of *Isaiah 22:22*. Thus:

> *And I tell you that you are Peter, and on this rock I will build my church, and the gates of Hades will not overcome it. I will give you the keys of the kingdom of heaven; whatever you bind on earth will be bound in heaven, and whatever you loose on earth will be loosed in heaven." (Matthew 16:18-19)*

> *"In that day I will summon my servant, Eliakim son of Hilkiah. I will clothe him with your robe and fasten your sash around him and hand your authority over to him. He will be a father to those who live in Jerusalem and to the house of Judah. I will place on his shoulder the key to the house of David; what he opens no one can shut, and what he shuts no one can open. (Isaiah 22:20-22)*

In this, as in several NT passages (*Luke 11:52; Revelation 3:7, 9:1, 20:1*), possession of a key implies authority to open or close a door. Thus, the church, by preaching the gospel, opens the door to the kingdom for those whom God has chosen and called. In one sense, all believers have this key in that all can and should make Jesus known, thereby opening the door of the kingdom to them. But it is properly also the authority of the local church by which new converts are baptised, receive the fullness of the Spirit, are brought into meaningful and active membership, and are discipled.

Satan is opposed to the church. Thus, there will always be attack upon and within her, not least by deception and division. Therefore Christ gave also the 'key' of church discipline, so that her leaders may be able to guard and protect her. In *Matthew 16:19* Jesus refers to 'binding' and 'loosing'. The same form of words is used in *Matthew 18:15-20* where the context shows that 'binding' means placing under church discipline, and 'loosing' means releasing from it. It seems reasonable, therefore, that *Matthew 16:19* also refers to church discipline. We conclude that in preaching the gospel and keeping watch over her own house, the church exercises the authority of the keys of the kingdom.

Handed over to Satan.

Sadly, there are sometimes instances of rebellion and difficulty in the church which must be dealt with by leaders, both for the sake of the individual concerned, and for the safety of that part of the body over which they have care. Jesus taught that there is a procedure which should be followed in the hope that the person concerned will accept the discipline of the church. If, however, that person remains obdurate and *refuses to listen even to the church, treat him as you would a pagan or a tax collector (Matthew 18:15-17).* Paul similarly, decreed that the church should *hand this man over to Satan, so that the sinful nature may be destroyed and his spirit saved on the day of the Lord (1 Corinthians 5:1-5; also 1 Timothy 1:20),* and that they should *expel the wicked man from among you (1 Corinthians 5:13).* Both Jesus and Paul are saying that such a person should be put out of the church and therefore back into the world, over which Satan rules.

On earth, as it is in heaven.

As with all devolved authority, that of the church is limited. Within the compass of the church the authority is all-inclusive, Jesus' use of the word 'whatever' (*Matthew 18:18-19*) implying that it covers individuals, relationships and situations. Nevertheless, this authority applies only in dealing with sin within the church, sin as defined by scripture. The church has no authority to define what is or is not sin, or to forgive sins in an absolute sense: these are God's prerogatives.

There remains an awesome feature of this use of authority. "Both *Matthew 16:19* and *18:18* use an unusual Greek verbal construction. It is best translated by the NASB, "Whatever you shall bind on earth *shall have been bound* in heaven, and whatever you shall loose on earth *shall have been loosed* in heaven. "Legitimate church discipline, therefore, involves the awesome certainty that corresponding heavenly discipline has already begun."[3] This passage shows as clearly as any in NT, the partnership of God and his church in action in bringing the kingdom to pass on earth as in heaven.

Authority within the church is not ....

Authority within the church, as in every other sphere of application, is limited to administering the will of God. Specifically, there is no room or place for authoritarian attitudes or 'heavy shepherding'. Jesus taught that the exercise of authority in his kingdom is to be in direct contrast to that seen in the world (*Mark 9:33-37; 10:35-45*). *"If anyone wants to be first, he must be the very last, and the servant of all."*

We were all sinners but we have been saved by grace, through faith, and that not of ourselves so that none may boast. Being saved we find that we are no longer our own, having been bought with a price. We are now slaves, bondservants. We have no rights of any kind, save that of access to the Father's throne. This is our status before God, in the church, and in each other's presence. It is not a statement about democracy, which is a wholly non-biblical concept, but of the way God has ordered his kingdom so that we shall know our utter dependency upon him.

Thus, anyone in any position of leadership, high or low, is no different from any other member of the body, save in the degree of anointing and delegated authority God has chosen to place upon that undeserving slave. He is called to serve the lost, the poor, the stupid, the arrogant and the unlovely, to share more than others in the sufferings of Christ, and to bear all in meekness and humility. He must give an account of his stewardship. His life must be one of greater self-discipline and separation to God than those of the ones he leads and serves. Like Paul, he may well be moved to cry: *Let no one cause me trouble, for I bear on my body the marks of Jesus (Galatians 6:17)*. He is to be pitied rather than envied.

Those who seek positions of leadership, or who are protective of their position and standing, do not understand these things, 'though in that they are in good company. Even as Jesus' earthly ministry approached its inevitable climax, his disciples were still jockeying for position.

To lead is to be pitched into a higher level of spiritual warfare. Wounds will be sustained, and sometimes casualties. Wounds bleed, and they bleed what is pumping through the veins and arteries. God expects the wounded leader to bleed worship. It is a precious, fragrant and costly sacrifice to God. John saw *a Lamb, looking as if it had been slain, standing in the centre of the throne (Revelation 5:6)*. Christ's work of suffering was finished at Calvary, yet it continues in his body, the church. Thus, the slain Lamb seen by John was still standing.

> Lamb of God, Holy One, Jesus Christ, Son of God
> Lifted up willingly to die
> That I, the guilty one, may know the blood once shed
> Still freely flowing, still cleansing, still healing
> I exalt you, Jesus my sacrifice
> I exalt you, Jesus my Redeemer and my Lord
> I exalt you, worthy Lamb of God
> And in honour I bow down before your throne.
> (Chris A. Bowater)

CHAPTER 5.

The Authority
of the
Believer and of Satan.

The believer's authority.

The believer's first encounter with God's authority is at the point of salvation. Having received God's word of truth, and having put our faith in Jesus, we are authorised to present ourselves to the world as sons of God.

Yet to all who received him, to those who believed in his name, he gave the right (exousia = authority) to become children of God. (John 1:12)

For he has rescued us from the dominion (exousia) of darkness and brought us into the kingdom of the Son he loves. (Colossians 1:13)

We are no longer sinners, but saints. We have been snatched out of Satan's power (*exousia*), our sins are forgiven, we have been made righteous, able to stand in the Father's presence, and kingdom authority has been conferred upon us. Under the Spirit's direction, we may act on his behalf, within the limits of our delegated authority. Glory to God!

Authority in Jesus' name.

All believers have authority to use the name of Jesus in prayer requests. Its similar to having a signed blank cheque. Thus:

> *I will do whatever you ask in my name, so that the Son may bring glory to the Father. You may ask me for anything in my name, and I will do it. (John 14:13-14)*

In scripture a name is a reflection of that person's character, so by praying in character with Jesus we are praying in his name. This is the true meaning of *ask in my name*. Its not just a phrase we tack onto the ends of our prayers because we're supposed to: 'In Jesus' name, Amen'! Its not a formula; its about praying out of the heart of Jesus because all true prayer starts in heaven.

Abiding (remaining, dwelling) in him and being saturated with his words means that we shall view every situation from his perspective rather than our own. The Spirit of Jesus lives within us, and the Spirit *knows the thoughts of God (1 Corinthians 2:11)*. To the extent that we are listening to and are obedient to the Spirit, we will know what he is thinking, we shall *have the mind of Christ (1 Corinthians 2:16)*, and thus we shall ask the Father for the things Jesus would have us ask for in our circumstances. What we then ask is in keeping with the character of Jesus.

Authority over all the works of the Evil One.

Much of what is given above about the authority of the church applies to the individual believer.

Thus, each believer has authority over all the works of the Evil One, including the power to bring the gospel into dark places, to heal and deliver, to see the devil flee at a word, to encourage and build up. Moreover, Jesus himself encourages us in the fight of faith, and in the warfare to which we have been born in the kingdom:

To him who overcomes I will give the right to eat from the tree of life, which is in the paradise of God. (Revelation 2:7)

To him who overcomes and does my will to the end, I will give authority over the nations ..... just as I have received authority from my Father. (Revelation 2:26-27)

Thus, those who learn to stand in and make effective use of the kingdom authority that is theirs in this present age, will be rewarded with Eden-like life, and a share in Christ's throne. They will reign with him. Hallelujah!

All of which is true and wonderful, but the fact is that many Christians, whilst believing and accepting these things, still struggle with day to day issues, for two reasons. (1) An awareness of sin and sinfulness, plus a gut feeling that 'all this stuff can't apply to me if I'm like this'. (2) Being unclear about the boundaries of their authority over their own lives. To what extent do I have authority over my own life as a saint? In what areas do I have freedom of action? Contrary to common belief, the Bible gives clear objective guidelines.

We now address these two issues, first clearing the ground by appreciating precisely what authority Satan has in the life of a Christian.

(1) Satan's authority.

God has never placed mankind under Satan's authority. However, Satan is head of a counterfeit kingdom of darkness in which he rules over all who are not in God's kingdom, both angels and men. Thus, the intention of evangelism amongst the unsaved is *to open their eyes and turn them from darkness to light, and from the power (exousia) of Satan to God (Acts 26:18; Luke 1:79).*

It is sometimes said that when Adam and Eve fell for the serpent's lie, Adam lost his authority over the earth to the serpent/Satan *(see Revelation 12:9)*. Certainly there were consequences: Adam and Eve were ejected from the garden and from imtimacy with God, and the whole earth was put under a curse *(Genesis 3:17-18)*, but the text makes no mention, or even implication, of a transfer of authority. Moreover, the serpent itself was cursed by God. Nothing in this account, therefore, in any way reduces or compromises God's authority over the earth. There was no transfer of authority from Adam to the serpent/Satan. Indeed, scripture declares unequivocally that: *The earth is the Lord's, and everything in it, the world and all who live in it (Psalm 24:1).* *"Every living soul belongs to me" (Ezekiel 18:4).*

Satan is described, *inter alia*, as *the prince of this world (John 12:31; 14:30; 16:11), the ruler of the kingdom of the air (Ephesians 2:2), and Beelzebub (= Lord of the flies!) the prince of demons (Matthew 12:24).* In using terms such as *the prince of this world,* or *the god of this age (2 Corinthians 4:4)*, or in stating that *the whole world is under the control of the evil one (1 John 5:19)*, scripture does not imply that Satan legally rules the world, only that he has authority over all who are not in God's kingdom. Christ's kingdom is being established upon earth and, at the end of the age, will be fully revealed on this planet. Satan has been comprehensively defeated by Christ and therefore cannot succeed in making this world his own, either now or at some future time.

Falling under Satan's authority.

All who have entered God's kingdom by repentance and faith in Jesus as Son of God, are no longer under Satan's authority, but under that of Christ and of the church. The believer has been made holy, righteous, and he need not sin. He is now a saint, not a sinner, but he soon discovers that he is, nevertheless, a saint who sometimes sins. This does not affect his position before God in that he remains a saint and is still within the kingdom, but in yielding to temptation over some issue, he has submitted to Satan in preference to God: he has, therefore, no authority over the Evil One in that context. In scripture this situation is treated using the concept of light versus darkness.

Physical light is electromagnetic radiation of wavelength 400 to 750 nanometers. It can be detected and focused by the human eye, and its information content assessed and interpreted by the brain. Spiritual light is the presence of God, who illuminates our spirit by contact with his Spirit. *The spirit of a man is the lamp of the Lord (Proverbs 20:27 NASB). Jesus said: "I am the light of the world" (John 8:12 & 9:5). He is the true light that gives light to every man (John 1:9).* Having received this light, we are to live by it, seeking understanding and wisdom, much as the brain processes the received stimulus of physical light.

For God, who said, "Let light shine out of darkness," made his light shine in our hearts to give us the light of the knowledge of the glory of God in the face of Christ. (2 Corinthians 4:6)

The Psalmist knew that *the entrance of your words gives light (Psalm 119:130)*, and God's first recorded act on this still formless planet was to speak physical light into it *(Genesis 1:3)*. The Psalmist had found God's word to be *a lamp to my feet and a light for my path (Psalm 119:105)*. Jesus, the living word of God said: *"Whoever follows me will never walk in darkness but will have the light of life" (John 8:12)*. Physical light has a dual nature: it is both a continuous wave, and discrete particles, called photons. Spiritual light is both *logos* and *rhema*, the general word of God and the specific word for the moment.

God's kingdom is the kingdom of light. In scripture, spiritual darkness is the absence of God and his kingly authority. Darkness, and the kingdom of darkness, are where Satan rules in his authority. Where God's authority is obeyed, there is light. Where there is rebellion and sin, there is darkness. Satan has legal access wherever there is darkness, even the darkness that still exists in the believer's heart. Therefore, Jesus warned his disciples:

See to it, then, that the light within you is not darkness. Therefore, if your whole body is full of light, and no part of it dark, it will be completely lighted, as when the light of a lamp shines on you."
(Luke 11:35-36)

Do not give the devil a foothold. (Ephesians 4:27)

Where there is sin, Satan rules legally, and the believer has no authority over him.

**Satan has legal access wherever there is darkness,
even the darkness that still exists in the believer's heart.**

Light and darkness cannot co-exist. Therefore, Isaiah's response to his vision of God's glory: *"Woe to me!" I cried. "I am ruined! For I am a man of unclean lips, and I live among a people of unclean lips, and my eyes have seen the King, the LORD Almighty" (Isaiah 6:5).* And that of Peter: *"Go away from me Lord, I am a sinful man" (Luke 5:8).* Sadly, some prefer darkness to light.

> *This is the verdict: Light has come into the world, but men loved darkness instead of light because their deeds were evil. Everyone who does evil hates the light, and will not come into the light for fear that his deeds will be exposed. But whoever lives by the truth comes into the light, so that it may be seen plainly that what he has done has been done through God." (John 3:19-21)*

> *This is the message we have heard from him and declare to you: God is light; in him there is no darkness at all. If we claim to have fellowship with him yet walk in the darkness, we lie and do not live by the truth. But if we walk in the light, as he is in the light, we have fellowship with one another, and the blood of Jesus, his Son, purifies us from all sin. (1 John 1:5-7)*

> *Where can I go from your Spirit? Where can I flee from your presence? ... If I say, "Surely the darkness will hide me and the light become night around me", even the darkness will not be dark to you; the night will shine like the day, for darkness is as light to you. ..... Search me, O God, and know my heart; test me and know my anxious thoughts. See if there is any offensive way in me, and lead me in the way everlasting (Psalm 139:7, 11-12, 23-24).*

An army compromised by enemy infiltration, by spies and traitors, will at best have limited success in battle, and may be altogether defeated. Therefore, Jesus warned: *"How can anyone enter a strong man's house and carry off his possessions unless he first ties up the strong man? Then he can rob his house"* (Matthew 12:29). Holiness, the state of living in complete submission to God's will, is the first of two keys to success in spiritual warfare. Yes, God can and does use us successfully in spiritual warfare in our imperfection, but for the higher, strategic-level work of taking cities and nations, the only complete protection against the enemy is humility and transparency before the One who sees and knows all, even the secret thoughts of our hearts.

The limited authority of demons.

Demonic authority and power is limited by God. It could hardly be otherwise, for Satan himself is under God's judgement. Nothing in scripture suggests even that demons can read our thoughts although, of course, God can (*Psalm 139:2, 4, 23; Isaiah 55:8; 66:18; Matthew 9:4*), and Satan could do to Job only what God allowed (*Job 1:12 & 2:6*). Equally, Satan could sift Peter *like wheat* only because God permitted it for a redemptive purpose (*Luke 22:31-32*). Demons drag themselves around trailing *everlasting chains* (*Jude v6*), and can be dismissed at a word by any citizen of the kingdom of heaven who is submitted to God and understands kingdom authority (*James 4:7*).

The Christian need not sin, but he does so because the flesh life, the carnal self-pleasing nature, which was nailed to the cross with Christ, is not always reckoned to be as dead as it actually is. Our sins are sometimes the result of yielding to demonically-inspired temptation or activity, but often they are simply the product of the still-active flesh life. More significantly, behind our sins lie heart attitudes and mind sets from which verbal and physical acts of wickedness and violence draw their energy. How much license does Satan have in this scenario?

The NT shows plainly that God expects his saints to learn how to be overcomers. Such is possible only by having some enemy to overcome. God requires that his people learn warfare (*Judges 3:2*). Hence, it follows that Satan is not prevented from testing us with temptations and attacks, although even here God watches over us, ensuring that we are not overwhelmed. As parents we expose our children to situations of increasing challenge and danger as they grow, so that they may be fully trained for adult life. God treats us similarly.

> *No temptation has seized you except what is common to man. And God is faithful; he will not let you be tempted beyond what you can bear. But when you are tempted, he will also provide a way out so that you can stand up under it. (1 Corinthians 10:13)*

God's purpose in allowing attacks upon us is always redemptive, and always because he loves us too much to leave us as we are. He will have us grow up into holy maturity and therefore, from time to time, he may allow Satan to 'sift' us in some specific and limited way so that we may see something about ourself that needs to be changed. We see a classic case of this in the life of the apostle Peter (*Luke 22:31-34; 54-62*).

Jesus specifically warned that Satan was actively involved in what was about to happen in Peter's life. Following Jesus' arrest, Peter three times denied that he knew him. Strange that, because the gospels reveal Peter otherwise as a man of courage and boldness, outspoken, impulsive. But the point is, Peter had an image to maintain. One of the inner group of three apostles closest to the Master, the only one who had walked on water, physically strong, and a natural leader, there was no way he was going to fail. That pride, unrecognised by Peter, was Satan's tripwire. God allowed Satan to attack on that point so that Peter might see what was in his own heart. Bitter repentance followed and, after his resurrection, Jesus took care to restore Peter in full view of the other disciples, 'though even then Peter was inclined to be irritable. Pentecost changed all that!

Conclusion.

The picture of Christian life that emerges from this study is of being under the loving protection of God who is committed both to us, and to changing us from one degree of glory to another (*2 Corinthians 3:18*). We do not face Satan and this world unprotected.

We *are under* the shadow of his wings, we *are* shielded by his power (1 *Peter* 1:5), his love and grace *are* poured out upon us, yet he exposes us to the trials, temptations, and dangers of this world in common with all mankind, so that we may learn to live in total dependence upon him, being purified from the effects of the flesh life, secure in him who alone is our righteousness. The key to this is intimacy with him.

He who dwells in the shelter of the Most High will rest in the shadow of the Almighty. I will say of the LORD, "He is my refuge and my fortress, my God, in whom I trust." Surely he will save you from the fowler's snare and from the deadly pestilence. He will cover you with his feathers, and under his wings you will find refuge; his faithfulness will be your shield and rampart.

You will not fear the terror of night, nor the arrow that flies by day, nor the pestilence that stalks in the darkness, nor the plague that destroys at midday. A thousand may fall at your side, ten thousand at your right hand, but it will not come near you. You will only observe with your eyes and see the punishment of the wicked.

If you make the Most High your dwelling— even the LORD, who is my refuge—then no harm will befall you, no disaster will come near your tent. For he will command his angels concerning you to guard you in all your ways; they will lift you up in their hands, so that you will not strike your foot against a stone. You will tread upon the lion and the cobra; you will trample the great lion and the serpent.

"Because he loves me," says the LORD, "I will rescue him; I will protect him, for he acknowledges my name. He will call upon me, and I will answer him; I will be with him in trouble, I will deliver him and honour him. With long life will I satisfy him and show him my salvation." (Psalm 91)

(2) The will of God in the believer's life.

Authority is given by God so that his will may be done on earth. Hence, for authority to be discharged properly, his will must be known. Specifically, I must know his will for me as an individual. This goes beyond simply obeying his commands - servants do that. It proceeds to sharing his heart so that his will may be known and understood.

> *I no longer call you servants, because a servant does not know his master's business. Instead, I have called you friends, for everything that I learned from my Father I have made known to you.*
> *(John 15:15)*

> *Then he said, "Here I am, I have come to do your will."*
> *(Hebrews 10:9)*

Therefore, Paul prayed for the Colossian Christians, *asking God to fill you with* **the knowledge of his** *will through all spiritual wisdom and understanding. And we pray this in order that you may live a life worthy of the Lord and may please him in every way: bearing fruit in every good work, growing in the knowledge of God. (Colossians 1:9-10)*

God commands:
(1) that we love God above all others, and our neighbour as yourself because *all the Law and the Prophets hang on these two commandments. (Matthew 22:36-40)*

(2) that we love one another as he has loved us - Trinity love! *(John 15:12);*

(3) that we obey him *(Matthew 28:20, etc)*

(4) that we pray *(Matthew 26:41; Luke 11:2, 18:1; Colossians 4:2-3; 1 Thessalonians 5:17; 1 Timothy 2:8).*

(5) that we are active in evangelising, discipling,
        and sharing our faith *(Matthew 28:18-20; Philemon v6).*

To these commands may be added particular matters which are either specifically declared by the apostles and others to be the will of God for us[1], or are implied as being so.

1. It is God's will that we be saved.

*This is good, and pleases God our Saviour, who wants
all men to be saved and to come to a knowledge
of the truth (1 Timothy 2:3-4). See also 2 Peter 3:9.*

2. It is God's will that we be Spirit-filled.

*Therefore do not be foolish, but understand what
the Lord's will is. ..... Be filled with the Spirit.
(Ephesians 5:17-18)*

3. It is God's will that we be sanctified.

*It is God's will that you should be sanctified.
(1 Thessalonians 4:3)*

4. It is God's will that we be submissive.

*Submit yourselves for the Lord's sake to every
authority instituted among men: whether to
the king, as the supreme authority, or to governors,
who are sent by him to punish those who do wrong
and to commend those who do right. For it is God's
will that by doing good you should silence the
ignorant talk of foolish men. (1 Peter 2:13-15)*

5. It is God's will that we live by faith.

*Without faith it is impossible to please God.
(Hebrews 11:6)*

6. It is God's will that we seek his face.

*If my people who are called by my name, will humble
themselves and pray and seek my face ....
(2 Chronicles 7:14).
Also Psalm 37:7, Jeremiah 33:3, Matthew 7:7, etc.*

7. It is God's will that we suffer.

... the sufferings of Christ flow over into our lives ... (2 Corinthians 1:5)

For it has been granted to you on behalf of Christ not only to believe on him, but also to suffer for him. (Philippians 1:29)

So then, those who suffer according to God's will should commit themselves to their faithful Creator and continue to do good.
(1 Peter 4:19)

These objective commands and statements of God's will are to form the framework of every believer's life. Alongside them we must place the many other detailed biblical instructions which cover the home and outside life and conduct of those who are citizens of the kingdom of God. So where does that leave us when facing decisions such as: 'What work should I chose?', 'Whom should I marry?', 'Where should I live?'. Do I have the authority to make those decisions?

Authority over our own wills and lifestyles.

Scripture talks of both predestination and freewill. Both concepts are there and are to be held in tension. On the one hand, God has not designed us as automata, whose lives are wholly predetermined. We do not run on rails! On the other hand, there is no such thing as absolute freedom: all mankind is intended to live within the boundaries of God's laws. However, I believe God has made us as individuals so as to enjoy our characters. Thus, we have considerable authority and freedom of action within the framework of God's commands and his will as outlined above. A key scripture in this context is *Acts 5:1-11.*

A married couple, Ananias and Sapphira, sold some land and gave the proceeds to the church, foolishly contending that they had gifted the whole sum whereas, in fact, they had reserved a portion for themselves. The only point that concerns us here is Peter's comment:
Didn't it belong to you before it was sold? And after it was sold, wasn't the money at your disposal?

In handling wealth we need to be aware that we are not owners, but stewards (*1 Chronicles 29:15*), and that God prospers us so that we shall be able to bless others with our excess. That said, we have freedom of action.

In respect of decisions in the area of marriage and relationships, Paul likewise indicates that we have wide-ranging freedom. *The man who has settled the matter in his own mind, who is under no compulsion but has control over his own will ... this man also does the right thing (1 Corinthians 7:36-38)*

These are but two areas of life in which we have authority over our own actions. The general issue has been extensively reviewed by Garry Friesen[2], who offers the following conclusions.

Principles of decision making.
1. In those areas specifically addressed by the Bible, the revealed commands and principles of God (his moral will) are to be obeyed.

2. In those areas where the Bible gives no command or principle (non-moral decisions), the believer is free and responsible to choose his own course of action. Any decision made within the moral will of God is acceptable to God.

3. In non-moral decisions, the objective of the Christian is to make wise decisions on the basis of spiritual expediency.

4. In all decisions, the believer should humbly submit, in advance, to the outworking of God's sovereign will as it touches each decision.
"The more we understand the revealed will of God, the more clearly we will understand the unrevealed will of God. Do what you know you should do, and you will receive guidance concerning what you don't yet know." (Selwyn Hughes)

Authority in the family: husbands & wives.
Wives, submit to your husbands, as is fitting in the Lord. Husbands, love your wives and do not be harsh with them. (Colossians 3:18-19)

Submit to one another out of reverence for Christ. Wives, submit to your husbands as to the Lord. For the husband is the head of the wife as Christ is the head of the church, his body, of which he is the Savior. Now as the church submits to Christ, so also wives should submit to their husbands in everything. Husbands, love your wives, just as Christ loved the church and gave himself up for her .... In this same way, husbands ought to love their wives as their own bodies. He who loves his wife loves himself. .... However, each one of you also must love his wife as he loves himself, and the wife must respect her husband. (Ephesians 5:21-25,28,33)

The key verse is *Ephesians 5:23* and it needs particularly careful handling. Its exegesis turns on a proper understanding of the word 'head' (Greek: *kephale*). In English this word often carries the figurative meaning of 'authority over', but this is not true of all languages (French and German, for example). In the secular Greek of NT times, *kephale* never carried the meaning of 'authority over', and the same can be shown to hold for its NT uses.[3]

In scripture "the controlling organ is not the head but the heart (Gk: *kardia*)". The head serves the body in many ways, "but the heart is the seat of the will, thought, motivations, and desire. In the NT it is the heart that wields authority over human beings and their behaviour, not the head."[3]

Verse 23 reads: *For the husband is the head of the wife as Christ is the head of the church, his body, of which he is the Savior.* Headship here is associated with Christ's function as Saviour. For the sake of the church whom he loves, Christ *gave himself up for her.* Thus, his headship is seen to be that of servanthood, as indeed he had explained to his disciples.

Jesus called the Twelve and said, "If anyone wants to be first, he must be the very last, and the servant of all" (Mark 9:35). Hence, the submission of husband and wife referred to by Paul is one of mutual service, just as Christ sets the example by serving the church sacrificially. It follows that headship within marriage, as in the church, is one of servanthood. Christ's teaching on this issue is very clear.

Jesus called them together and said, "You know that those who are regarded as rulers of the Gentiles lord it over them, and their high officials exercise authority over them. Not so with you. Instead, whoever wants to become great among you must be your servant, and whoever wants to be first must be slave of all. For even the Son of Man did not come to be served, but to serve, and to give his life as a ransom for many." (Mark 10:42-45)

This verse (*Ephesians 5:23*) is commonly taken as an excuse for male dominance. We now see that this is unbiblical, and that the error arose from reading the content of the English word 'head' into the Greek word *kephale* which bears no such meaning.

Husbands are to relate to their wives as Christ does to the Church. Out of the most amazing depth of love, he humbled himself first in heaven and in obedience came to earth to share our life. On earth he again humbled himself to the Father's will, accepting death on a cross (*Philippians 2:1-11*). The purpose was that all mankind should be saved (*John 3:16, 1Timothy 2:3*). Everyone who belongs to Christ and has a personal relationship with him knows something of the astonishing grace with which he has dealt with us, the patience, and the total absence of any pressure or condemnation. Everything he does in our lives is positive and in love and for our benefit. He is to us the source of every good thing. More, he never criticises or condemns. This is how a husband is to relate to his wife!

The scriptural meaning of 'head' in respect of a man's function in marriage is that he is to be the source of blessing to his wife, devoted to serving her in every possible and necessary way. Domination, heaviness, and authoritarian attitudes are unscriptural.

And if that is not enough to convince husbands, let us recall that all of this family-related teaching falls within the general principle of *Ephesians 5:21*. Within marriage, husband and wife are to be submitted to each other, serving each other's needs in love and gentleness. This is easy to write but may be hard to establish, especially when a couple become Christians later in life. In marriages in which the wife "wears the trousers", true peace and mutual fulfilment will come only with God's order for them.

Christ's intent is to bring the Church to a state of perfection, *to make her holy, cleansing her by the washing with water through the word, and to present her to himself as a radiant church, without stain or wrinkle or any other blemish, but holy and blameless.* It follows, then, that a husband's first and most vital ministry is to his wife. He should be jealous for her spiritual progress, and do everything possible to ensure it. How? As Christ does for the Church, without pressure but leading by example, pursuing righteousness and Christ-likeness. The apostle Peter says much the same *(1Peter 3:1-7).* Above all, everything within marriage must be done in love.

Authority in the family: children and parents.

Children, obey your parents in everything, for this pleases the Lord. Fathers, do not embitter your children, or they will become discouraged. (Colossians 3:20-21)

Children, obey your parents in the Lord, for this is right. "Honor your father and mother"--which is the first commandment with a promise--"that it may go well with you and that you may enjoy long life on the earth. "Fathers, do not exasperate your children; instead, bring them up in the training and instruction of the Lord. (Ephesians 6:1-4)

Again, there is to be nothing heavy or domineering about parents. The aim is to bring children up in "the nurture and admonition of the Lord", and to lead by example in love, patience and peace. "Good advice", you may say, "but I wish you had had my child to deal with!" If the parents are relating as they should, nothing the child does should be able to drive a wedge between them. This is a vital first principle. Then by prayer, though the gifts of the Spirit, by the application of biblical principles of discipline and nurture, and with the help of the local church where needed, most situations can be brought under control.

Authority in the workplace: slaves and masters.

Slaves, obey your earthly masters with respect and fear, and with sincerity of heart, just as you would obey Christ. Obey them not only to win their favor when their eye is on you, but like slaves of Christ, doing the will of God from your heart. Serve wholeheartedly, as if you were serving the Lord, not men, because you know that the Lord will reward everyone for whatever good he does, whether he is slave or free. And masters, treat your slaves in the same way. Do not threaten them, since you know that he who is both their Master and yours is in heaven, and there is no favoritism with him. (Ephesians 6:5-9; also Colossians 3:22-4:1)

Read this as "employers and employees" and the passage immediately becomes relevant to modern society. You may even regard yourself as a "wage slave"! God calls us to work in all walks of life, so that we may be salt and light to our society.

I once worked in an organisation in which a senior person of a bitter and selfish nature cast a pall over the entire operation. Eventually, that person was replaced. The new appointee was a Christian. Within a very short time, joy and peace permeated the place, and it became a pleasure to go into work.

Paul teaches that we should treat our employers (even if it is a Government department!) with the same standards of probity and behaviour we expect in the Church. Equally, employers should behave likewise. Christ-likeness will colour every relationship we have, and everything we do, to his glory.

Authority in the community.

Everyone must submit himself to the governing authorities, for there is no authority except that which God has established. The authorities that exist have been established by God. (Romans 13:1)

Submit yourselves for the Lord's sake to every authority instituted among men: whether to the king, as the supreme authority, or to governors, who are sent by him to punish those who do wrong and to commend those who do right. (1 Peter 2:13-14)

These scriptures declare unequivocally that God is the source of all governing authorities: they are delegated by him to rule, they are his servants in that capacity, whether or not they acknowledge the fact, and therefore are to be obeyed. Their remit is to reward the good and punish the evil doer.

Cyrus, a Persian King, and certainly not a worshipper of Jehovah, is described as God's chosen 'shepherd' and 'anointed' one (*Isaiah 44:28, 45:1*), whose heart God moved (*Ezra 1:1*) to begin the restoration of his people Israel following their captivity in Babylon. Jesus taught the principle of civil obedience in commanding his fellow Jews to *"Give to Caesar what is Caesar's"* (*Matthew 22:21*); in paying the Temple tax (*Matthew 17:27*); and in responding under oath to the high priest's question during interrogation (*Matthew 26:63-64*).

Fine, but what if the ruling authorities are corrupt? Suppose that their laws or commands are contrary to scripture - what are we to do? The answer lies in understanding the difference between submission and obedience.

Submission and obedience.

Submission goes before obedience, because submission is a heart attitude, whereas obedience is a matter of conduct. In a Christian submission should be one of the constants of his lifestyle. In contrast, our obedience cannot always be total (except towards God), because whenever there is conflict between the demands of temporal authorities and those of scripture, *We must obey God rather than men (Acts 5:29).*

Submission is a heart attitude. It should be total.
Obedience is a matter of conduct. It may be partial.

Thus, should an order be given which clearly contradicts God's will, we are to be submissive in attitude to the person in authority because that person represents God's delegated authority, but disobedient to the order. Peter, for example, openly preached the gospel in Jerusalem in contradiction of an order of the Council, but submitted to being imprisoned for it.

CHAPTER 6.

Authority and character.

The distinction between spiritual and worldly authority.
The spiritual authority we are studying is given by God to those he has chosen and appointed for a specific purpose. It is a delegated authority, confined within clear boundaries.

The sole reason authority is conferred upon a man or woman by God is his sovereign will and choice. No-one earns or deserves anything from God. We have been rescued by him from certain death because of his great love. We are now his undeserving servants, and he can place upon anyone whatever responsibility he chooses. Therefore, no-one can boast of his delegated authority, or of what may be achieved by its exercise.

In fact, in the true servant who is in authority, there is a delightful contradiction. Although he may bear heavy responsibilities and be tightly focused upon them, there is at the same time an absence of consciousness of being in authority. Why? Because he is far more aware of being the little servant of an illustrious Lord, than of ruling his flock and standing over them.

His heart is to serve his people rather than to rule them, 'though in order to serve them he must also rule them. His senses are attuned to the Holy Spirit more than to his people. Others are attracted by the light within him, whilst being restrained by the anointing upon him.

This contrasts with worldly authority in which, as Jesus said, *"the rulers of the Gentiles lord it over them, and their high officials exercise authority over them. Not so with you. Instead, whoever wants to become great among you must be your servant, and whoever wants to be first must be your slave - just as the Son of Man did not come to be served, but to serve, and to give his life as a ransom for many" (Matthew 20:25-28).* The Christian in a position of authority is to be more aware of being under authority than of exerting it, knowing that authority is given him so that he may faithfully do the will of God. The worldly leader will commonly use his position for selfish ends, sometimes spectacularly so. Christian and, indeed sometimes other godly cultures, produce many who work in public administration and service, consciously serving the community rather than their own ends.

Committed to seek God's will.
Authority is given so that the will of God may be implemented. Therefore, a prime concern of the Christian in authority will be to know God's will in his situation, because he cannot act on God's behalf until he knows what is required. Unless the prophet stands *in the council of the Lord to see or to hear his word (Jeremiah 23:18),* he has nothing to say to the people, and neither does the preacher. The meek and humble in spirit, who seek God's face to know his heart and his will, are fit to handle his delegated authority.

Unwilling to defend himself.
In strict contrast to those in worldly authority, the Christian who bears God's delegated authority will not defend himself, because to justify oneself is to make that person your judge. God defends those he has anointed and appointed.

Preparation for authority.

Those who administer such authority faithfully have certain characteristics in common which readily distinguish them from others in the church who have raised themselves into leadership, or who have allowed themselves to be elevated by men.

Christ-likeness - the measure of authority.

All authority is from God (*Romans 13:1*). He confers it upon whom he chooses, but it is not a random process. God's will is that all grow up into maturity in Christ, but not all do. *Many are called but few are chosen (Matthew 22:14 KJV); Many get invited; only a few make it (The Message).* In other words, not all appreciate that the grace of God is a responsibility as well as a free and unmerited gift. It's the law of giving and receiving in operation: what we give determines what we get.

These truths lead to the conclusion that God's authority is given to those whose hearts are ready for it. Not that they will have been consciously working towards a position of authority, only that they have worked to establish a lifestyle of seeking God's face, of loving him for himself, and of submission to his will. In a word, they are pursuing Christ-likeness, pressing on *towards the goal to win the prize for which God has called me heavenwards in Christ Jesus (Philippians 3:14).* They are people who are surprised to have authority laid upon them, and who consider themselves unfitted for it. The measure of Christ-likeness is the measure of the authority granted, because to bear God's delegated authority is to represent God himself, acting as his ambassador.

> **The measure of Christ-likeness is the measure of the authority granted, because to bear God's delegated authority is to represent God himself**

Brokenness - pre-requisite for authority.

To do God's will implies having first submitted to his authority, since authority is given in order to implement his will. All who belong to Christ have, of course, bowed the knee to him, but we refer here to a deeper submission of heart and soul which only the Holy Spirit can affect. It is called 'brokenness'.

In the early stage of discipleship, it is often sin that must be dealt with primarily. Later, the Spirit calls us to deal with root causes which lie in the dead but still influential self-life. Whatever we may have of abilities, gifts, education and experience must all be laid on the altar. Natural traits which interfere with hearing God must go: the talkative and self-opinionated must learn to prefer his voice and his wisdom to their own.

Battles are fought and tears shed as self is submitted to God, but he who began a good work in us doesn't give up on us until the job is done (*Philippians 1:6*). We become sensitive to the whispers of the Holy Spirit, and to the least stirring of his presence, rather like a biscuit apparently intact on a plate but instantly revealing its brokenness as it is touched.

At a crisis point in his life, Jacob met with God and was broken. In consequence he was told that *as a prince hast thou power with God and with men (Genesis 32:28 KJV)*. That is still true. *Humble yourselves, therefore, under God's mighty hand, that he may lift you up in due time (1 Peter 5:6)*.
"The way up is down!" (Colin Urquhart)

God will have us sensitive to the whispers of his Holy Spirit, and to the least stirring of his presence.

Awareness of God's discipline.
A man (or woman) in authority has no authority of himself. He is not authorised to use his own initiative, but to implement God's will as revealed to him by the Holy Spirit. Anything outside that, either more or less, is an abuse of authority which God will deal with strictly.
Moses exceeded his authority when he struck the rock instead of speaking to it, commanding it to yield water for the thirsty Israelis (*Numbers 20:2-12*). God's judgement on Moses was to

prevent him from entering the promised land along with the rest of the nation, although he was permitted sight of it before he died. The implication is that Moses' life was prematurely shortened, although his presence with Elijah at Jesus' transfiguration (*Mark 9:2*) shows that his heavenly reward was unaffected.

God watches over his word to see that it is fulfilled (*Jeremiah 1:12*). Clearly, it must first be spoken faithfully, as was imprinted upon Ezekiel when he was commissioned as a prophet to the nations, and warned of the personal consequences of failing to speak what he was given (*Ezekiel 3:16-21*). The greater the authority conferred, the greater the strictness with which that person is dealt. God will have us tremble at his word (*Isaiah 66:2*).

> **The greater the authority conferred, the greater the strictness with which that person is dealt.**

Submissive to others.

God gives authority only to those whose hearts are submissive. That submission must be to man as well as to God. To *submit to one another out of reverence for Christ (Ephesians 5:21)* is not at all incompatible with bearing great authority. Indeed, God delights in using the most obscure and unlikely saints to speak words of awesome import into the lives even of those who seem to us to be great in the church. Many are the instances in which ministry depends upon not the solo personality, but upon two or more together, Paul and Barnabas, for example. Even Jesus submitted to John Baptist's ministry before entering upon his own.

> **God's pre-requisites for authority: a submissive heart and a teachable spirit.**

Sanctification - the price of authority.

There is a cost to authority. The greater the degree of authority, the greater the price. Following the untimely death of

Aaron's sons, Nadab and Abihu, because of their presumptuous offering of *unauthorised fire* before the Lord, there unfolds a most revealing sequel (*Leviticus 10*). First, through Moses, God emphasises that the point at issue is his holiness and the honour of his name. His word is to be obeyed precisely and implicitly: Nadab and Abihu had treated it carelessly, added their own interpretation, and had reaped the terrifying reward.

Secondly, Aaron, who had just seen two of his four sons die, was forbidden to follow the customary form of mourning, or even to grieve. Moreover, he was not to leave the Tent of Meeting or to accompany the family mourners or *you will die, because the Lord's anointing oil is on you*. What is happening?

The point at issue is not sin but sanctification. Aaron had not sinned and was in no way being punished. To mourn the death of a loved one is perfectly legitimate, but Aaron and his two remaining sons had been sanctified to the Lord as priests, to serve in his presence. They had to understand that:

(1) the closer a man draws to God, the stricter the obedience required; and
(2) to be sanctified means that things permitted to others are not permitted to me.

But that was under the old covenant. How does this incident translate to the new covenant of Christ's blood, under which all are priests to God, and all are sanctified? To understand this we need to appreciate the meaning of sanctification, because sanctification has a bearing on the exercise of authority.

To be sanctified is to be made holy, and the root meaning of holiness (Hebrew: *qodesh*) is 'separation to God'. Its' opposite, therefore, is not sinfulness but to be 'common' (Hebrew: *chol*), or 'ordinary'. Sanctification is the process of growth into Christ-likeness, the progressive separation of the believer to God. It begins at new birth when the believer is justified (a once-for-all change of legal status), and made holy. It continues throughout life. "It is an individual possession built up, little by little, as the result of obedience to the word of God (*John 17:17*), and of following the example of Christ in the power of the Holy Spirit."[1] It will be completed only at Christ's return, when we shall all bear the likeness of the man from heaven (*1 Corinthians 15:49*).

Justification[2]	Sanctification
Legal standing	Internal condition
Once for all time	Continuous throughout life
Entirely God's work	We co-operate
Perfect in this life	Not perfect in this life
The same in all Christians	Greater in some than in others

It is important to see that sanctification includes two elements of increasingly complete separation: (1) from the sinful ways of the flesh life; and (2) from legitimate and non-sinful things which nevertheless conflict with God's will for us. The point is illustrated perfectly by Jesus in his 'high priestly' prayer shortly before his arrest and trial. Praying for his disciples he said: *For them I sanctify myself, that they too may be truly sanctified (John 17:19).*

Plainly, for Jesus, *tempted in every way, just as we are—yet without sin (Hebrews 4:15),* there was no need of further separation from sin. Rather, his need of sanctification was to choose to obey the Father's will and go to the cross, rejecting the natural desire to hold onto life and all that it offered. By that choice, he opened the way for the Holy Spirit to come to all who received him by faith, *that they too may be truly sanctified.* Thus, the same principle is in operation as with Aaron. There is a requirement to decline something entirely legitimate in order to fulfil the will of God. How, then, does this apply to the Christian in a position of authority? Answer: exactly as it did for Aaron.

(1) The closer a man draws to God, the stricter the obedience required. Things that once seemed too trivial to notice now assume large proportions and must be dealt with. We see even that *all our righteous acts are like filthy rags (Isaiah 64:6).*

(2) As our fellowship with him deepens we discover that we are more than happy to forego entirely good things in order to seek his face, to stand in his council, and so to know and to do his will. Sleep is rejected in favour of nights of prayer; fasting becomes an indispensable feature of our lifestyle; we become willing to avoid even the appearance of evil (*1 Thessalonians 5:22*); perhaps to refrain from drinking wine, even though our Lord created it in bucketful's at a wedding, so that a weaker brother may not stumble. Like the holy vessels in the Jerusalem temple, we come to be reserved (almost) exclusively for God's use.

I am the LORD your God; consecrate yourselves and be holy, because I am holy. (Leviticus 11:44)

Be perfect, therefore, as your heavenly Father is perfect.
(Matthew 5:48)

The greater the degree of authority, the greater the price.
The price is sanctification.

Though I am free and belong to no man, I make myself a slave to everyone, to win as many as possible. .... I do all this for the sake of the gospel, that I may share in its blessings. (1 Corinthians 9:19,23)

In a large house there are articles not only of gold and silver, but also of wood and clay; some are for noble purposes and some for ignoble. If a man cleanses himself from the latter, he will be an instrument for noble purposes, made holy, useful to the Master and prepared to do any good work. (2 Timothy 2:20-21)

Authority with God.
Many are called to the largely hidden ministry of intercession. Often such people will have no recognised position or authority within their church, yet they have great authority with God. They stand before his throne, to worship, to hear and to see, to touch God's heart of love. Then they are able to pray with precision and authority. They act as midwives in God's kingdom. At their

word strongholds fall, ministries are transformed, principalities and powers of evil are torn down, even cities and nations impacted, often through the lives of others who may never even have heard of them.

Satan trembles before such saints, for they stand as Princes and Generals on the field of battle, unassailable in humility and selflessness. More than for most in the church, Christ is their life. They live to pray. They are in love with Christ and the Holy Spirit, and this is the source of their authority, their intimacy with the godhead.

Nevertheless, this, the purest exercise of authority delegated to man, is to be employed under the umbrella of the church's authority. Of course, this is not to limit the freedom of the individual intercessor, but to remind us that the ministry of intercession is part of the overall work of the local and wider church which is being directed by God through leaders chosen for that purpose. Thus, for example, it is now becoming widely recognised that evangelistic events are of little value unless the spiritual victory is first applied by intercession.

"Evangelism without intercession is an explosive without a detonator. Intercession without evangelism is a detonator without an explosive." (Reinhard Bonnke)

And he said, Thy name shall be called no more Jacob, but Israel: for as a prince hast thou power with God and with men, and hast prevailed. (Genesis 32:28 KJV)

Awareness of responsibility.
God delegates kingdom authority to his church, and having done so does not violate it. Thus, he waits for his people to develop an awareness of their responsibility to understand and operate in their delegated authority. He knows what we need even before we ask, but he waits for us to ask.

Authority and responsibility go together.

REFERENCES

Chapter 2
2.1. *New Dictionary of Theology*, S.B. Feguson & D.F. Wright (Eds), IVP, Leicester, UK, 1988.

2.2. *A Theology of the New Testament*, G.E. Ladd, Eerdmans, Grand Rapids, USA, 1979.

Chapter 4
4.1. *Readings in St John's Gospel*, W. Temple, Macmillan, Basingstoke, UK, 1968.

4,2. *Prophetic Vision*, No. 4, 1996, Eurovision Publications, 41 Healds Road, Dewsbury WF13 4HU, UK.

4.3. *Systematic Theology*, W. Grudem, IVP, Leicester, UK, 1994, p889-891.

Chapter 5
5.1. *Reckless Faith*, J.F. MacArthur, Crossway Books, Wheaton, Ill., USA, 1994, p189.

5.2. *Decision Making and the Will of God*, G. Friesen, Multnomah Press, Portland, Oregon, USA, 1980.

5.3 *Beyond Sex Roles* 2nd Ed., G Bilezekian, Baker Books, Grand Rapids, USA 1985.

Chapter 6
6. 1. Ref. 1.1.

6.2. Ref. 4.3, p746.

APPENDIX: definitions.
[W.E. Vine][1]

Humble (verb). [Gk. *tapeinoo* = to make low.]

Humility. [Gk. *tapeinophrosune*, from *tapeinos* = low lying, and *phren* = the mind.] Hence, lowliness of mind.

Meekness (noun). [Gk. *praütes*] "The meaning of *praütes* is not readily expressed in English" "Described negatively, meekness is the opposite to self-assertiveness and self-interest; it is equanimity of spirit that is neither elated nor cast down, simply because it is not occupied with self at all." *Praütes* has none of the connotations of weakness and timidity commonly associated with the English word 'meekness'. "The meekness manifested by the Lord and commended to the believer is the fruit of power."

Obedience. [Gk. *hupakoe*, from *hupo* = under, and *akouo* = to hear.] Thus, to be submissive to commands and to authority, to yield to another's will.

Submission. [Gk. *hupoeiko*, from *hupo* = under, and *eiko* = to yield.] Thus, submission is 'to yield to' another. Closely related to 'subject' and 'subjection' [Gk. *hupotasso*, from *hupo* and *tasso* = to arrange.] "Primarily a military term, to rank under".

1. *Expository Dictionary of Bible Words*, W.E. Vine, Marshall, Morgan & Scott, Basingstoke, UK 1981.

Further Reading

I give You Authority Charles H. Kraft, Monarch Books, Crowborough, England 1998.

SCRIPTURE INDEX

1Corinthians

14:17	29

1Corinthians

2:11	52
2:16	52
4:20	29
5:1-5	48
5:13	48
6:9-11	28
7:19	29
7:36-38	63
9:19,23	77
10:13	58
15:24	17
15:45	35
15:49	76
15:50	27

2Corinthians

1:5	61
3:18	59
4:4	54
4:6	55
10:5	29
10:8	44
13:10	32,44

Galatians

6:17	49

Ephesians

1:20-23	25
2:2	54
4:11-13	44
4:27	56
5:17-18	61
5:21	65,74
5:22-24	64
5:27	44
6:1-4	66
6:5-9	67

Philippians

1:6	73
1:29	62
2:6-11	22,25,28,65
2:8	24
3:14	72

Colossians

1:13	51
1:9-10	60
2:10	25
2:15	24
3:18-22	63,66,67
4:1-3	60,67

1Thessalonians

4:3-4	61
5:11	45
5:12-13	32
5:17	60
5:22	77

1Timothy

1:20	48
2:3-4	61,65
2:8	60
5:17	32

2Timothy

2:20-21	77

Titus

1:9	44
2:15	44

Philemon

6	60

Hebrews

1:9	25
2:14	24
3:13	45
5:8-9	23,28,35
4:15	24,76
10:7	28
10:9	60
11:6	61
13:17	32

Further copies of this title and copies of
the other two books by David M. Adams
can be purchased on-line from

www.theway.co.uk

or by contacting

Harvest Fields Distribution
Unit 17 Churchill Business Park
Churchill Road
DONCASTER
DN1 2TF
UK

Tel: +44 (0)1302 367868
Fax: +44 (0)1302 361006